Little
Princess
Name:

Little
Princess
Name:

Little
Princess
Name:

Little
Princess
Name:

Little
Princess
Name:

Little
Princess
Name:

Little
Princess
Name:

Little
Princess
Name:

Little
Princess
Name:

Little
Princess
Name:

Little
Princess
Name:

Little
Princess
Name:

Little
Princess
Name:

Little
Princess
Name:

Little
Princess
Name:

Little
Princess
Name:

Little
Princess
Name:

Little
Princess
Name:

Little
Princess
Name:

Little
Princess
Name:

Little
Princess
Name:

Little
Princess
Name:

Little
Princess
Name:

Little
Princess
Name:

Little
Princess
Name:

Little
Princess
Name:

Little
Princess
Name:

Little
Princess
Name:

Little
Princess
Name:

Little
Princess
Name:

Little
Princess
Name:

Little
Princess
Name:

Little
Princess
Name:

Little
Princess
Name:

Little
Princess
Name:

Little
Princess
Name:

Little
Princess
Name:

Little
Princess
Name:

Little
Princess
Name:

Little
Princess
Name:

Little
Princess
Name:

Little
Princess
Name:

Little
Princess
Name:

Little
Princess
Name:

Little
Princess
Name:

Little
Princess
Name:

Little
Princess
Name:

Little
Princess
Name:

Little
Princess
Name:

Little
Princess
Name:

Little
Princess
Name:

Little
Princess
Name:

Little
Princess
Name:

Little
Princess
Name:

Little
Princess
Name:

Little
Princess
Name:

Little
Princess
Name:

Little
Princess
Name:

Little
Princess
Name:

Little
Princess
Name:

Little
Princess
Name:

Little
Princess
Name:

Little
Princess
Name:

Little
Princess
Name:

Little
Princess
Name:

Little
Princess
Name:

Little
Princess
Name:

Little
Princess
Name:

Little
Princess
Name:

Little
Princess
Name:

Little
Princess
Name:

Little
Princess
Name:

Little
Princess
Name:

Little
Princess
Name:

Little
Princess
Name:

Little
Princess
Name:

Little Princess
Name:

Little
Princess
Name:

Little
Princess
Name:

Little
Princess
Name:

Little
Princess
Name:

Little
Princess
Name:

Little
Princess
Name:

Little
Princess
Name:

Little
Princess
Name:

Little
Princess
Name:

Little
Princess
Name:

Little Princess
Name:

Little
Princess
Name:

Little
Princess
Name:

Little
Princess
Name:

Little
Princess
Name:

Little
Princess
Name:

Little
Princess
Name:

Little
Princess
Name:

Little
Princess
Name:

Little
Princess
Name:

Little
Princess
Name:

Little
Princess
Name: